DEAR GHOSTS,

Other Books by Tess Gallagher

DEAR GHOSTS,

Poems by

Tess Gallagher

Graywolf Press
SAINT PAUL, MINNESOTA

Publication of this volume is made possible in part by a grant provided by the Minnesota State Arts Board, through an appropriation by the Minnesota State Legislature; a grant from the Wells Fargo Foundation Minnesota; and a grant from the National Endowment for the Arts, which believes that a great nation deserves great art. Significant support has also been provided by the Bush Foundation; Target, with support from the Target Foundation; the McKnight Foundation; and other generous contributions from foundations, corporations, and individuals. To these organizations and individuals we offer our heartfelt thanks.

MINNESOTA
STATE ARTS BOARD

NATIONAL
ENDOWMENT
FOR THE ARTS

Published by Graywolf Press
2402 University Avenue, Suite 203
Saint Paul, Minnesota 55114
All rights reserved.

www.graywolfpress.org

Published in the United States of America

ISBN 1-55597-443-0

2 4 6 8 9 7 5 3 1
First Graywolf Printing, 2006

Library of Congress Control Number: 2005938149

Cover design: Christa Schoenbrodt, Studio Haus

Cover art: Alfredo Arrequín, *Bitterns' Moon*

ACKNOWLEDGMENTS

Grateful acknowledgments are made to the following publications where poems have appeared:

American Poetry Review: "The Red Devil," "Dear Ghosts," and "Little Match Box"

Artful Dodge: "The Dogs of Bucharest," "Lady Betty," "Moon's Rainbow Body," "Emanation of the Red Child," and "Oil Spot"

Clackamas Review: "The Rooster Crows"

Columbia Poetry Review: "Eternal" and "I Asked That a Prayer"

The Grove Review: "Irish Weather," "Unspoken," and "Black Beauty"

The Kenyon Review: "Offering," "Heart-Mirror," and "The Violence of Unseen Forms"

New Orleans Review: "My Unopened Life" and "Death's Ink"

The Salt River Review: "Orange Sutra" and "The Women of Auschwitz"

The Sun: "Sixteenth Anniversary," "Remains," and "With Setouchi-san in Kyoto"

Van Gogh's Ear: "Weather Report," "Emanation of the Red Child," and "*Sah Sin*"

Witness: "She Wipes Out Time"

"My Unopened Life" won a Pushcart Prize and appears in the 2006 *Pushcart Prize XXX Best of the Small Presses*.

"Urgent Story" first appeared in *My Black Horse: New and Selected Poems,* published in Britain by Bloodaxe Books, 1995.

"Sugarcane" first appeared in *Portable Kisses,* published in Great Britain by Bloodaxe Books, 1992, 1994, 1996.

"Behave" first appeared in *Passing the Word: Writers on Their Mentors,* edited by Jeffrey Skinner and Lee Martin, published by Sarabande Books, 2001.

"Choices," "Not a Sparrow," "*Sah Sin,*" and "Heart-Mirror" appeared in *America Zen: A Gathering of Poets,* edited by Ray McNiece and Larry Smith, published by Bottom Dog Press, 2004.

"I Never Wanted to March" appeared in *Poets Against the War,* edited by Sam Hamill, published by Nation Books, 2003.

"Not a Sparrow," "Choices," "Weather Report," and "Bull's-Eye" appeared in *Contemporary Northwest Poets,* edited by David Biespiel, published by Oregon State University and Ooligan Press, 2006.

"Choices," also was selected for inclusion in the 2005 Washington Poets Association Member Anthology.

"Choices" will appear on coffee mugs at Starbucks across the country.

So many people contributed to this book, I name them with trepidation. If I miss you, maybe I can add you into the next edition! I want especially to mention those who actively went over the manuscript: Greg Simon, Ted Stein, Holly Hughes, Chana Bloch, my former secretary and great friend Dorothy Catlett, and especially Katie Ford who braved the ramparts with close readings and essential kindness. Their gifts are contributions at a level where even thanks is a kind of ragged attempt to express the blessings of right companioning. Harold Schweizer's words of encouragement and rereadings buoyed me up at crucial stages. Josie Gray, who never complained to find me ranging the house during the early morning hours, working on the book in the silence of a sleeping house, deserves the thanks of love. Jill

Ginsberg did important duty as a sweet dragon lady who kept reminding everyone I was working, and thereby made room for me to be out of active correspondence. This preserved a great measure of peace in which to collect myself during a period of strenuous demands, both physically and spiritually. Bill Stull and Maureen Carroll gave solace, expert advice, and were mainstays in friendship. To Susan Lytle and Alfredo Arreguín, who opened their home and hearts to me for three major periods of convalescence; I feel the enduring and immense gratitude of long friendship become kinship. I wish to thank also oncology nurse Kathy Ringo, Dr. Georgiana Ellis, Dr. Ben Anderson, Debra Jarvis, Barbara Morris, the expert crew in Blood Draw, and all those at SCCA in Seattle who rallied around me during my sojourn with them. To Carmen Perkins, the crack shot at Olympic Medical Center, I give a deep bow of thanks. Dr. Mike Silverstein and Dr. Kari Haronaka were there with me at all the challenging medical junctures and I greatly thank them for the balance they loaned me. Immensely important: Haruki and Yoko Murakami came from Tokyo to see me near the start of my chemotherapy and greatly encouraged me. Recovery from my various surgeries would not have proceeded so well without the help of Loraine Lovejoy Evans and her sister, Tonni Lovejoy. Further, I wish to thank Dr. Clare Bertucio, Dr. Heath Foxlee and John Engstrom at Olympic Medical Cancer Center. Bonnie, Wendy, Edie, Helene and the nurses at Olympic Medical Center Short Stay Unit have ministered each week to me in my hometown. To my near and dear neighbor and friend, Alice Derry, who heard some of these poems before anyone, and who buoyed me up by coming to tea and to my weekly infusions and just laughing with me—thank you! Holly Hughes kept in weekly touch and arranged our Winter Retreat with Thich Nhat Hanh at Deer Park Monastery. Holly with John Pierce, Molly and Thad McManus visited at important junctures and lifted me greatly in spirit. Alan and Joyce Rudolph gave shelter and delight. Teresa Olson, my hairdresser, came to the house to cut my long braid before chemotherapy, then shaved my head. Later she took my portrait in Buddha Alcove. Rijl Barber, my niece, let me mind Tiernan Barber, my grandnephew, at intervals, which added much joy. My sister, Stephanie Barber, my brothers Morris Bond and Tom Bond—each stayed by me in their own ways at important times, which made me feel secure and loved. My mother, Georgia Morris Bond, whom I was blessed to be able to care for in my home this past year before her death on September 9, 2005 kept me in the deep time of her past. She has been a great and overweening cherishing. The eight children of Josie Gray have welcomed and included me. Eileen McDonagh and Dymphna Gray changed my life utterly with their many kindnesses over more than thirty years. Ciaran and Deirdre Carson opened their home to me in Belfast on numerous occasions, made music, cooked meals, shared their children, especially Mary. Sean and Sheila McSweeney inspired me with art, songs, and great meals. My translators around the world who've become dear friends: Hiromi Hashimoto, Riccardo Duranti, Christine Rimoldy, Asadollah Amraee, Juri Hruby; my mentor and beloved teacher, Margaret Matthieu, now passed away, is with me throughout. Sylvia Kind and Dr. Bob Marks, also deceased, are important ongoing presences. Larry and Sarah Berk, Maya Nahum and Alain Sarfati, Lela Hilton and Jake, Anna Manildi and Jack Galloway, Peter Stein, Kamish and Kashi Wali, Tom and Liz Luce, Susan Powell, Fran McConnell, Shawn Montcastle, Barbara Sorkes and Talia Jade, Kate Noonan, Nita and John Hamrick, Jay and Raku Rubin, Ann Albritton, Keiko Hara, Pat Henry, Irving Hashimoto, Vicki Lloid and Madeline DeFrees. To Drago Stambuk for helping to bring me to his homeland of Croatia and for welcoming me in Cairo. To Jakucho Setouchi-san, my spiritual sister in Kyoto. To all, bountiful thanks. And Ray, always Ray.

to the ghosts
in and out of the flesh
who accompany me
with such tenderness, such ferocity

CONTENTS

i

ii

iii

vii

. . . black butterflies of the general soul,
join me to those who are missing, those who sleep
like hives of wild honey, who sleep with their
sweetness intact like a blue door sure and firm
in the swift corridors of the night.

from "Dear Ghosts,"

i

to be neither separated from words nor
obstructed by words

Wang Duanshu
(*Daughters of Emptiness,*
translated by Beata Grant)

My Unopened Life

lay to the right of my plate
like a spoon squiring a knife, waiting
patiently for soup or the short destiny
of dessert at the eternal picnic—unsheltered
picnic near the mouth of the sea
that dares everything forgotten to huddle
at the periphery of a checked cloth spread
under the shadowy, gnarled penumbra
of the madrona.

Hadn't I done well enough with the life
I'd seized, sure as a cat with
its mouthful of bird, bird with its
belly full of worm, worm like an acrobat of darkness
keeping its moist nose to the earth, soaring
perpetually into darkness without so much as
the obvious question: why all this darkness?
And even in the belly of the bird: *why
only darkness?*

The bowl of the spoon
collects entire rooms just lying there next
to the knife. It makes brief forays into
the mouth delivering cargoes of ceilings
and convex portraits of teeth
posing as stalactites of
a serially extinguished cave

from whence we do nothing but stare out
at the sea, collecting little cave-ins of

3

perception sketched on the moment
to make more tender the house of the suicide
in which everything was so exactly
where it had been left by someone missing.
Nothing, not even the spoon he abandoned
near the tea cup, could be moved without
seemingly altering the delicious
universe of his intention.

So are we each lit briefly by engulfments
of space like the worm in the beak of
the bird, yielding to sudden corridors
of light-into-light, never asking: *why,*
tell me why
        all this light?

NOT A SPARROW

Just when I think the Buddhists
are wrong and life is not mostly suffering,
I find a dead finch near the feeder.
How sullen, how free of regret, this death
that sinks worlds. I bury her near
the bicycle shed and return to care for
my aged mother, whose suffering
is such oxygen we do not consider it,
meaning life at any point exceeds
the price. A little more. A little more.

That same afternoon, having restored balance,
I discover a junco fallen on its back, beak
to air, rain pelting the prospect. Does
my feeder tempt flight through windows?
And, despite evidence, do some
accomplish it?

Digging a hole for the second bird, I find
the first gone. If I don't think "raccoons"
or "dogs," I can have a quiet, unwitnessed
miracle. Not a feather remains.
In goes the junco. I swipe earth over it,
set a pot on top. Time
to admit the limitations of death as
admonition.

Still, two dead birds in an afternoon
lets strange sky into the mind: birds flying
through windows, flying through

earth. Suffering must be like that too: equipped
with inexplicable escapes where the mind
watches the hand level dirt over the emptied grave
and, overpowered by the idea of wings,
keeps right on flying

SAH SIN

I found the hummingbird
clutched in torpor
to the feeder on the day
my student from long ago
appeared. I sent him into
the house and tried to
warm it, lifting my blouse
and caching it—(as I'd heard
South American women do)
under a breast.

It didn't stir, but I held it there
like a dead star for a while
inside my heart-socket
to make sure, remembering the story
of a mother in Guatemala
whose baby had died
far from home. She pretended
it was living, holding it
to her breast the long way
back on the bus, so no one
would take it from her before
she had to give it over.
When the others on the journey
looked across the aisle
they saw only a mother and
her sleeping child, so tenderly
did she hold the swaddled form.

Miles and miles we flew
until I knew what that breast
was for when the form
of your not-there arrived. We
were impenetrably together
then, as that mother and child
must have been, reaching home at last,
her child having been kept alive
an extra while by the tender glances
of strangers.

Inside, my student and I found
a small cedar box
with a Nootka salmon
painted onto its glass lid.
I told him of the dead
hummingbirds people saved
in their freezers because
they found them too beautiful
to bury. We made a small mausoleum
for *Sah Sin* under the sign
of the salmon, so the spear of her beak
could soar over death a while longer.
Next we propped the box
on the window ledge
facing out toward the mountains.

Then we went on about
our visit. My student
had become famous in the East
for his poems. Now he was

a little bored with being
a poet. He asked some questions
about what I might be
writing—courteously, as one
inquires about someone
not considered for a while.
I made a pot of tea
and served it in the maroon cups
the size of ducks' eggs
so it would take
a long while to drink. Fame.
It was so good to sit
with him. He seemed
to have miraculously survived
every hazard to make his way
to my house again.

Sah Sin is the Nootka word for hummingbird.

A STROKE OF SKY

It was so sudden.
A stroke of sky.
A few impending clouds
where windows and doors,
where corridors had been. And people.
All those unfinished stories,
suddenly finished. So sundered
they spire up in us
when we least expect it.

We became taller
from the eyebrows up, a weariness
in the voice. Our fabled American buoyancy,
our save-the-day vigor slumped
to urgent reciprocity—like relatives
in a quarrelsome family
who see each other only at funerals,
and don't need to
speak, just nod and press
each other's hands, language
compressed to gesture so it is like
a tall shuttered street
fringed with pent-up light
leaking into the dark until, silence to
silence, some internal murmur forces us
to commune.

It was so sudden. Soon
we were sitting in cafes, talking
like refugees on our front porches, our speech

Bogart-clipped, unsheltered without
its hat. What didn't we know
about fate, about smiling wistfully,
purporting to live for the moment?

Overnight we became European—
without world wars pounding us
into cellars. With Hiroshima and
Nagasaki cauterized in black-and-white
documentaries as: *they-made-us-do-it.*
(Cut-to-bomb-in-profile. Bomb-in-bib
looking baby-faced, full on.)

At the diner, grateful
for the salutary: *How would you like your eggs?*
Lilting *sunny side up*
or *over easy,* touchstones of a time before
the unthinkable assumed its savvy shroud,
until we coveted the loss of even one person,
known and loved, asking that direness
pierce us crucially.

Our inner plea: not to be absent
from pain through the tourniquet
of irony, denial's tepid bath water
that poisons the soul's aquifer. Yet, overnight
we were European. We practiced sighs,
cocking an eyebrow. Tossed a mocking
grimace, but with charm. On a planetary scale
and with history looking on, it didn't
take much to bring us to this dim

Midwestern bus stop.
This little island
of blackly green nostalgia.

The suddenness of it!
Could this be a sign of hope?
Or is that an American question.

SAYONARA, BABY

My accent, she says, is Canadian
or maybe Irish. She's Californian
by way of New York. I apologize falsely
for my counterfeit amalgam. Proximities
enlist me. Canadian English blows across
the strait or laps ashore as I sleep. I absorb language
the way the fir tree at my window licks up
sea breeze with giant drooping wands.

Over thirty years sojourning with the Irish—their music,
poetry, stories. Their political malaise. Such
intermittently hyphenated collaboration
adds a Celtic lilt when an Irish friend visits.
Why wouldn't there be slippage?—my ear a burr
that clings as word-hover, syllables extending even
the air as pleasantly foreign, until a contrail
thins to sky, and the inaudible arabesque
of thought-sound lingers, fades, then isn't.

What to make of those childhood recesses
spent perfecting an English accent
with my best friend Molly. Did poetry
begin there, casting off constrictions of class
and small-town sameness for the burl and arch
of Dickens? O to be next door to the x in *exotic,*
the tantalizing wave savoring some opposite
shore! At Okasan, the Japanese-Korean cafe
run by the Korean, I overhear the cook
from Trinidad shout: "Sayonara, Baby!"
when his favorite waitress goes off shift, his

companionable salute parting the general din
of conversation with that happy shark
of verbal soul. He is that shade of olive
that seems to whisper. Brown eyes
glistening under lashes that brush the curtain
as he passes from kitchen to dining room.

He takes lunch with the dishwasher,
telling how after 9/11
some locals tried to bash
him headless with a baseball bat when he stopped
for gas. "I'm the one went to jail," he says, "the bat
in my hands when the cops came.
Could have done damage, oh yes, damage,
for sure. And me loving flowers
and dogs. Never like that. But mad, so
mad I had to be taken away. My Trinidad—
taken over, thirty-one times. English, French, Dutch,
French, et-cet-er-a. You think I don't
know how to boogie?" He slides into my booth
and we just look.

Being born American stains, sustains me.
We just look.

To apologize for hometown bullies, as if birthright
were ownership, no good to either of us.
Then some smiling comes that says
it's provisionally okay to go back
to being "free," but with a dart of fear
at the center.

Like the koto, we're tuned like-unalike
to set music satisfyingly on edge, prying syllables
from their complacent ledges
and yes, slanting Canadian-Irish or
Japanese-Korean-Caribbean if that's what it takes
to lift the eyelid of each word
as it leaves the plush silence of the mind
to join the broken-open accents of rain
falling skylight-staccato
above the cook.

And, because glass stops an overflow of sky,
the rain-telegraph keeps getting through—its urgency
so like the midnight flag
of a chewing gum I bought in Tokyo, *BlackBlack,* its
ginger-ginseng scald
keeping daylight awake—
BlackBlack on glass, *BlackBlack,* until the mouth
goes dry and you spit it out,
however you can—the mouth, so ahead of us
at choosing its moment.

for Clayton

THE DOGS OF BUCHAREST

Their invisible city of cries and threats
builds in the air, thrives briefly, then
falls away to a fresh oblivion.
What do they protect so fiercely, as if
they had several lives to sacrifice?
Yesterday a mastiff the size of a small pony
bashed against the wire mesh
of its narrow yard just because we were passing.
While we ate fish at the restaurant—a meal
stolen from those who can't afford an egg—
the dogs began another alarm, their chuffing
like black shovels full of earth tossed
into an open grave that is everywhere
when fear is the predominant language.

We ate anyway, two poets disguised
by a room crowded with businessmen,
cell phones pressed to their ears: *communication,
not communion,* Liliana says. But it's
catching. We want to phone someone too. We ask
the surly waitress with eyes like a drowned cat
if we can use the restaurant phone,
but she answers no.
Ditto for the male waiter who passes too close
where we work on our translations
of each other's poems, trying to convert
one heart's currency to another
without spiritual loss.

And shouldn't we bark and show
teeth in this place where so much is against
what we want the world to be? Not men
clamoring across borders, across continents,
buying and selling the cheap labor
of their countrymen and women—converting,
for profit, little into less, so
the deft hands of the bread-makers glimpsed
through an open doorway can never keep pace
with a nation that survives on bread.

Ask to borrow that man's cell phone, I tell Liliana,
and she does. He hands it over, after dialing
for us. It rings and rings in an empty house.
We pass it back, dead thing.
No one expects our call. But in that empty room
where the telephone rang and rang
poems were written; the poet's son studies
for exams in a fan of light
in the corner. Last evening friends
drank champagne made from raspberries,
told of the pilgrimage to Medjugorje
where the Virgin Mother appeared.

Strange, Aurelia said, *how the pilgrims
weren't looking at the sky when they got to
that mountaintop. They scoured
the ground for small stones
to carry away, to extend her blessing.
But only boulders were left, or sand*—too much
or too little.

Aurelia hands me the small rust-colored stone
wrapped in the handmade linen
of her grandmother—*So it won't seem too lonely,*
too strange—to give you a bare stone.
In my palm, her gift of belief
and safe passage. I pass it hand to hand
around the table where each one examines it,
an oval face carrying its tiara of light.

ii

We are drunk on poetry and can't find our car
when we leave the restaurant.
We stumble in the labyrinth, passing
the same newly painted metal fence with the warning:
"*Danger of Electrocution.*" No one believes it, but
no one tests it either.
I pick up a stone and fling it
until it clangs against the gate
like a Chinese temple gong. A dog ignites
behind the fence, its rage monumental.

We too are deranged with the freedom of friendship
and the little Dutch cigars we smoked
intending to stain, to penetrate the lungs
of those silk-shirted men in the restaurant.
And probably they are no worse
than killer bees, doing what they do
with the special ferocity of opportunists
anywhere. They will never read our poetry, that
is certain.

But the oxygen of poetry is its own happy
contagion, even if our voices reach only as far as
the next ear in a room where Helene has sent
three roses she couldn't afford; Paula has painted
dream horses in a frozen forest of white
mesticcini trees—horses that shatter
our autumn air—one's head arched, carrying
a burden we can't see, the other raised
in an inaudible, cadaverous whinny. Jagged
Brancusi boulders border their prancing, sharp
as the steel prongs of the fence
surrounding the former waiter's house, a man
who now buys and sells with impunity the fur
of Romania's animals, growing so rich,
he's just another unsavory bandit,
a man no one dares stop
as entire populations of forest creatures
are turned into coats and hats and rugs.

iii

The poorly paid professor of chemistry,
my temporary neighbor across the yard, Rodica,
a widow, lives her life out in one room,
a shared kitchen, the bath a floor
below. How valiantly the light-into-light glow
of her candela flickers, even in daylight.
Its insistent halo in the window
is a beacon after another insomniac night, sleep
riddled with the inflamed skirmishes
of wild dogs against captive dogs, as if

their disconsolate howls warned of thieves
more invidious than even these half-starved dogs
could intimidate.

I go to my borrowed window
that faces Rodica's casement, stand gazing out
to drink hazelnut coffee cached
in my luggage. Suddenly, she appears,
throws back her curtain, lifts
her bare white arm and waves—shyly,
sweetly, like a small girl, then strongly,
with an upward thrust that is unmistakable.
My arm lifts of itself, as if it has always known
the language of arms—two widows
greeting, saluting each other. Just that. A sign
across this chasm of life—where
to recognize the suffering of even one other,
that alchemy of reception, fortifies against despair.

Then that inevitable, necessary moment
when we drop our arms,
turn our backs to the window. Do
the next ordinary thing.

for Liliana Ursu, for Rodica, for Aurelia

ii

Time to put our arms
around each other's waists—my man, my woman, my
unapproachable dream.

from "Dear Ghosts,"

CHOICES

I go to the mountain side
of the house to cut saplings,
and clear a view to snow
on the mountain. But when I look up,
saw in hand, I see a nest clutched in
the uppermost branches.
I don't cut that one.
I don't cut the others either.
Suddenly, in every tree,
an unseen nest
where a mountain
would be.

for Drago Štambuk

Irish Weather

Rain squalls cast sideways,
the droplets visible
like wheat grains
sprayed from the combine.
As suddenly, sunshine.
If a person behaved
this way we'd call them
neurotic. Given weather, we gust
and plunder with only
small comment: it's
raining; sun's out.

BRUSHING FATE

On the road from Ballindoon, night
of no moon, haze-your-breath night,
driving the hedge-high gauze of turns
like plunging eyes-first
down a worm hole. Sudden silvery slump
of badger caught in headlight magnification
by which night diminishes
and badger looms.

How I need you, badger, so the world
can again be strange enough
to save. Beautiful forlorn of winter,
and Josie's foot down hard
on the brake. Badger does not so much
as glance, as if his errand in the night could not
have been broken by any force, its current so strong
bearing him and us
away from that hollowed-out

moment, cave-of-never in which life is
everlasting and renewed by simply going on
past averted calamity. Our late night meal
of potatoes, fish and cauliflower
tasting better because badger did not die.
The night younger too, sitting by coal fire
in the borrowed cottage
overlooking Lough Arrow, me
trying to explain, because Josie asks, the ruin
of young love by war, my first husband

having come home some-sort-of-alive
from Vietnam thirty years ago,

carrying in his pocket shrapnel dislodged
from his plane, memento of one fate
having spared him
so another could put him down.
He was made use of, as we do
make use, and are forever shamed and stupid and young,
until night gets smaller, illuminating
two figures—a man, a woman,
whose one-time embrace still has the power
to brush hearts past midnight,
as if we'd saved them a little
to be in love ourselves, and worse than war
careening the darkness, worse
than death and forgetting
about to come toward
us. In that loophole-moment

badger let us have again the freezing stars
of an Irish morning. Only in that slip-knot time
of near-miss could those we are torn from
loom again, and in the starkness
of lost love, could you see me
afresh, Josie, and hesitate crucially
for him you never knew.

for Lawrence Gallagher and Josie Gray

After Looking at Property
in a Busy Irish Town

Lovely to return to the countryside.
Bird song. Eating breakfast outside
in my nightgown—sure no one
is arriving. Brown bread. Strong tea.
In the bath: whiskey-colored water
from the river. Ceilings sixteen foot high.
The stone hearth wide enough
to sleep on. Bird song.
Within walking distance of fresh eggs
from Brian and Marese's hens.
Blackberries to pick along the way, hedged
in white thorn, each berry a black-eyed
serpent glistening, not caring
if it's picked or withers on the vine.

The smug realtor shows us
a small bungalow
in town facing an electric
terminal. Then a badly designed
jumble of rooms abutting
a farmer's field. We know
instantly, despite what he says,
the field is sure to become
building sites when the price
is right.

Bird song. My lamb
grazing in electric green grass
at Ballindoon.

SUGARCANE

Some nights go on in an afterwards so secure
they don't need us, though sometimes one exactly
corresponds to its own powers of elemental tirelessness.
A prodigious heaviness comes over it that upswings it
into taking us, like the seizure knowing is,
back into its mouth. One blue-violet night in Hawaii during
the Vietnam War pinions me against

the war's prolonged foreboding as I relive it yet
in the preposterous homecoming the generals arranged
for their men on R & R in that meant-to-be paradise. Wives
flown in to bungalows and beach-side hotels, their suitcases
crammed with department-store negligees for conjugal trysts
that seem pornographic now in their psycho-erotic
rejuvenation of the killing. But he

was my husband. And I was glad he hadn't gone down
in a craze of flak in some widow-maker out of Da Nang
zigzagging over to Cambodia to drop its load. Glad
my government had a positive view of sexual continuity,
wanted its men in loving arms at their war's halftime.
We would meet, as some would not. Seven months gone—
daily letters, tapes and that telepathic hotline reserved
for saints and gods, except when women's wartime
solicitations to their mates usurped all tidy elevations.
But what did

those heavenly bodies, those angel currents, make of so much
heavy panting and suppositional boudoir?
Or of the homeward-yanking fantasies; interspersals
with napalm, sniperfire, firebombing, mines—the dead,
the wounded lifted out by helicopter?
I would see you in and out of khaki
again. Was early to the island, tanning a luxurious khaki
into my sallow in a luminescent bikini after months
working the dawn shift on a medical ward.
But the night is tired of its history
and doesn't know how we got here. Children

are what it wants. Though we didn't know it, no amount of
innocent gladness of the young to meet again on earth
would bring them back. Nor could they be revived
in the glower of long rain-shattered afternoons as we labored
to push ourselves back into each other.
They were gone from us, those children.
As if disenfranchisements like this were some mercurial,
unvoiceable by-product of the country's mania, its payment
in kind for those flaming children

we took into the elsewhere. There was so much to spare you
I had to overuse loving as balm, a cauterizing
forgetfulness to prise you to me. Maybe the exuberance
of our stretching all the way to first-love, that *always*
to each other, allowed our lack its comfortless posture,
and we were given respite in which a quiet light
thought us human enough to slough off its breath-saddened
anguish. And then I saw you

made new again in moonlight. Not as yourself, but as
more entirely made of pain in its power
of always usurping what might also
be true. As I was true in moonlight, preparing to meet you,
lifted by the raw gaiety of my brother's shipmates
taking shore leave the night before you touched down,
the gleeful carload of us emptied into a field
because I'd never tasted sugarcane.
Breaking off the chalky stalks,

my juiceless sucking and licking the woody fiber
in darkness, the flat way it discarded me, as if another, greedier
mouth had been there first. Then the young man's voice,
my hand with his around it lifted, so he tore with his biting
the stalk I held, squeezing my hand until the full pressure
of his jaw passed into me
as what was needed for sweetness to yield.

And since sweet pressure is all I gave—that boy's
unguarded kiss in moonlight was yours, was any god's invitation
to how we'd meant our love to close us,
close, in a little rest, allowing
that sweet scythe of unfoulable kindred tenderness, before
the rest. That biting down on us.
The heavy pressure that demands its sweetness as it mouths
and sucks, until it finds us with its love-letting teeth.

Knives in the Borrowed House

Don't sharpen them.
Expectation, more dangerous
than any blade.

I Have Never Wanted to March

or wear an epaulet. Once I walked
in a hometown parade to celebrate
a salmon derby. I was seven, my hair in
pigtails, a steel flasher strapped diagonally
across my chest *bandolier*-style
(in Catalan *bandolera* from *banda*—band
of people—and *bandoler* meaning bandit).
My black bandit boots were rubber
because here on the flanks of the Olympics
it always rains on our parades.

I believe I pushed a doll buggy.
I believe all parades, especially military
parades, could be improved if
the soldiers wore *bandoliers* made to attract
fish, and if each soldier pushed a doll buggy
inside which were real-seeming babies,
their all-seeing doll-eyes open
to reflect the flight of birds, of balloons
escaped from the hands of children to
hover over the town—higher than flags, higher
than minarets and steeples.

What soldier could forget
collateral damage with those baby faces
locked to their chin straps? It is
conceivable soldiers would resist
pushing doll buggies. Bending over
might spoil the rigidity of their marching.

What about a manual exhorting the patriotic
duty of pushing doll buggies? Treatises
on the symbolic meaning would need to be
written. Hollywood writers might be of use.
Poets and historians could collaborate,
reminding the marchers of chariots, of
Trojan horses, of rickshaws, of any wheeled
conveyance ever pulled, pushed or driven
in the service of humankind.

I would like, for instance, to appear
in the next parade as a Trojan horse. When
they open me I'll be seven years old.
There will be at least seven of me
inside me, for effect, and because it's
a mystical number. I won't understand
much about war, in any case—especially
its good reasons. I'll just want to be pushed
over some border into enemy territory, and
when no one's thinking anything except: *what
a pretty horse!* I'll throw open myself
like a flank and climb out, all
seven of me, like a many-legged spider
of myself. I'll speak only
in poetry, my second language, because it
is beautifully made for exploring the miraculous
ordinary event—in which an alchemy
of words agrees to apprentice itself to the possible
as it evades the impossible. Also poetry

doesn't pretend to know answers and speaks best
in questions, the way children do
who want to know everything, and don't believe
only what they're told. I'll be seven
unruly children when they open me up,
and I'll invite the children of the appointed enemy
to climb into my horse for a ride. We'll be secret
together, the way words are
the moment before they are spoken—
those Trojan horses of silence, looking for a border

to roll across like oversized toys
manned by serious children—until one horse
has been pushed back and forth
with its contraband of mutually pirated children
so many times it will be clear to any adult watching
this unseemly display, that enemy territory
is everywhere when anyone's child is at stake, when
the language of governments is reduced to ultimatums,
when it wants to wear epaulets
and to march without
its doll buggy.

But maybe an edict or two could be made
by one child-ventriloquist through the mouth
of the horse, proposing that the advent of atrocities
be forestalled by much snorting, neighing, prancing and
tail swishing—by long, exhausted parades
of reciprocal child-hostages who may be
rescued only in the language of poetry
which insists on being lucid

34

and mysterious at once, like a child's hand
appearing from under the tail
of the horse, blindly waving to make sure that anyone
lined up along the street does not submit entirely
to the illusion of their absence, their
ever-squandered innocence, their hyper-responsive
minds in which a ladybug would actually fly away,
with only its tiny flammable wings,
to save its children from the burning house.

WEATHER REPORT

The Romanian poets
under Ceausescu, Liliana
said, would codify opposition

to the despots in this manner: because
there was no gas and they were cold, everyone
was cold, all they had to do was write

how cold it is . . . so cold . . . and their
readers knew exactly what was meant.
No one had to go to jail
for that.

Liliana, in the dead of night
writing her poems
with gloves on.

I think I'll take off my gloves.
It's freezing in here.
There's a glacier pressing on my heart.

ETERNAL

"So what," he says. He's
fifteen, has seen heads
blown from bodies—legs,
arms, entrails strewn.
"So what." He is clutching
a rifle, leveling his
no-man's-land black eyes
into the camera.

He's been fighting for years.
Something mirthful
plays at the corners
of his mouth. If the camera
turned into a gun
he would empty his rifle
into the cameraman
with his last breath.
And even as he breathes it
he won't believe
it's his last.

He hasn't belonged
to himself perhaps ever.
A last breath is what the living
worry about. He isn't a thing
like that. He's a soul
who craves bullets. Looking into him
is like staring into
a small clenched sun.

And so you finally see him,
dulled on his haunches
by your shadow. And you become
for a moment some vagabond god,
and you bless him. That's
what gods are for.

Okay. Now withdraw
the god. Withdraw
the blessing. That's how it's done.
The emptying out
of several words, two
souls, many gods.

Only human.
Bullet. Bullet. Bullet.
Dead. Only dead.
Are you with me?

iii

How can one find passage on the ship
of compassion?

Miaohui
(*Daughters of Emptiness*,
translated by Beata Grant)

The Women of Auschwitz

were not treated so well as I.
I am haunted by their shorn heads,
their bodies more naked for this
as they stumble against each other
in those last black-and-white
moments of live footage.

Before she cuts the braid
Teresa twines the red ribbon
bordered with gold into my hair.
The scissors stutter against the thick
black hank of it, though for its part,
the hair is mute.

When it was done
to them they stood next to each other.
Maybe they leaned
into each other's necks afterwards. Or
simply gazed back with the incredulity
of their night-blooming souls.

Something silences us.
Even the scissors, yawing at
the anchor rope, can't find their sound.
They slip against years as if they were bone.
I recall an arm-thick rope I saw in China
made entirely of women's hair, used to anchor
a ship during some ancient war
when hemp was scarce.

At last the blades come together
like the beak of a metallic stork,
delivering me into my new form.
The braid-end fresh and bloodless.
Preempting the inevitable,
Teresa uses the clippers to buzz off
the rest. Breath by plover-breath, hair
falls to my shoulders, onto the floor, onto
my feet, left bare for this occasion.

As the skull comes forward,
as the ghost ship
of the cranium, floating
in its newborn ferocity, forces through,
we are in no doubt: the helm
of death and the helm of life
are the same, each craving light.

She sweeps the clippings onto the dust pan
and casts them from the deck
into the forest. Then, as if startled awake,
scrambles down the bank
to retrieve them, for something live
attaches to her sense of hair, after
a lifetime cutting it.

I am holding nothing back.
Besides hair, I will lose toenails, fingernails,
eyelashes and a breast to the ministrations
of medicine. *First you must make
the form*, Setouchi-san tells me, explaining
why the heads of Buddhist nuns are shaved.
The shape is choosing me, simplifying,
shaving me down to essentials,
and I go with it. Those women
of Auschwitz who couldn't choose—
Meanwhile the war plays out
in desert cities, the news shorn of images
of death and dismemberment.

I make visible the bare altar
of the skull.
Time is deepened. Space
more intimate than
I guessed. I run my hand over
the birth-moment I attend sixty years
after. I didn't know the women
would be so tender. Teresa takes my
photograph in Buddha Alcove, as if to prove
the passage has been safe. Holly, Jill, Dorothy,
Alice, Suzie, Chana, Debra, Molly and Hiromi offer flowers
and a hummingbird pendant, letting me know
they are with me. My sister
is there and Rijl.

I feel strangely gentled, glimpsing
myself in the mirror, the artifact
of a country's lost humility.
My moon-smile, strange and far,
refuses to belong to the cruelties
of ongoing war. I am like a madwoman
who has been caught eating pearls—softly radiant,
about to illuminate a vast savanna, ready
to work a miracle with everything left to her.

LADY BETTY

Given the death sentence for murder,
she saved her life by becoming executioner
at Roscommon Jail, Ireland, 1740.

So there you stood
giving the hangman's yank,
the rope attached to
someone's neck, a neck not
unlike yours—fleshy, strung
to heart and brain. One report
thought you deserved a movie.
Indeed, the harder to sort truth,
the stranger the myth we make.
For instance, was it your husband or
your son you murdered?

In a cleansing of the general soul
the town used your deed
as their reprisal. For no recompense
but life, you accepted their burden
as yours, to feel each time you took
a life—the updraft of the death
you'd escaped. More than others, did
you experience the body as
thing, disposable, its animation
gradually twitched away, then stilled?

What had your husband done so "murderer"
became you? At Roscommon Jail's inception
matrimonial crimes of the era:
beatings in drunkenness, servitude
of the bed, accusations of the usual

domestic sort. "Who was she hanging?"
asks Marese, chopping onions
for shepherd's pie. Putting down the knife,
"She must have known everyone she hanged."
A lantern flares in the greater darkness.
What heart was in her? Did she steel it or
let it flow?

Retribution. Strange idea.
Yet she agreed to serve in exchange
for life. Did she wear lost lives, or
after a while, was it just another day's
work? Did she earn the right to walk
the town? If so, did the townsfolk meet her
in the shops, a specter in human form?

I think they stepped aside. Made way for
dignity in reverse. Lady Betty.
For she relieved them of much, and if
she thought less of them, it's unlikely she gave
sign. Complicity is like that:
a not-so-secret bond, accomplished without
tearing the fabric. She is rent and upright
when I think of her.

On the radio an American voice,
a boss-executioner, admits *how wrong*
it all seems, no matter the crime. He's
a Texan. No clemency there.
They are dying often in Texas.
But in Roscommon town of not so long ago

Lady Betty is stepping high, going
home to her children, whose arms
around her knees must have broken
doorways into corridors of unwitnessed
mercy where she walks yet
in only that rectitude.

OFFERING

Before hunting season
Josie prunes the apple trees.
Leave the branches where they
fall, I say, having seen at dusk
the tensile lips of the deer
reaching up.

Day into dusk and
the sign of their feasting.
Nearest thing to joy, the limbs
over days gradually stripped
to a many-antlered thicket
on the ground.

Not to witness necks
bent to forage—
somehow a right communion
in a time when, even to
exchange glances, plea
to plea, might harm
an inner complicitous reaching.

When shots on the mountain
crack the stillness, their sacrifice
must now include us.

LITTLE MATCH BOX

And if there were two moons,
who would sleep when one
passed before the other
and took it in
on its dark side? Wouldn't
some extra light ray out
around the sustaining one?
Wouldn't you sense
the two in one, even if you'd
never seen them parted?

Sometimes a glory
is just that—a guessing-into
the seen, noticing
the fringe of presence
when it comes, trying to match
its fervency by something
as tangible, something
only you are equal to.

FIRE STARTER

The seen caresses the unseen.
Two eagles, like twin palms in shadow-play
flex an opening in sky, heavily gain
the pitch of my roof.

It's WWII. My father
is a pipe-fitter in the Bremerton shipyards.
For a year I am an only child running
into the winter glare. But before my father goes
to the shipyard, my mother
lets me see him, in recollection, leave the bed in darkness
to work another job.

He slips from warmth not to wake us.
Soon, like a thief who belongs, he enters,
one after the other, the neighborhood houses, before
the families are up. He gathers
what he needs to lay the fire
in each stove, then strikes a match
to set it going, so when they rise
from sleep, the house will have the chill off
and a fire crackling. Such work is his
because these southern transplants
don't yet know what will catch fire
in the damp of hemlock, fir and alder.

My young father, newly arrived himself
from coal mines and cotton fields
to the Northwest, carrying fire, hearth to hearth,
in a time when no one locks their doors.

House to house he clears ashes, crumpling
news of war: *June 6, 1944.*
ALLIES INVADE EUROPE.
In a calculated toss, he
adds kindling split the night before, builds
the loose crisscross cedar scaffolding
for fire to climb, mindful that even flames
must breathe—leaving space for breaths,
in his absence, to be drawn.
He does this before I know what fire is, how it
arcs back to caves and clearings,
our ancestral huddlings.

I am nearly a year old.
The first nuclear bomb is being readied to drop
on Hiroshima and, *for good measure,* Nagasaki.
It is something of which my father
will never speak—so far beyond his ken,
the use of people, their homes, as incidental
combustibles. What news of Nazi ovens
he had, or what he thought, I do not
know. Only that Europe
was always over there,
and he didn't need to see it, asking me later
Are you sure you have to go over there?

My father on his knees
in the sleeping house, trying not
to wake the babies, and beneath
the dull clang of wood against metal
the muffled sounds of lovemaking, or

the low murmur of the night's dream-cargo
exchanged between husband and wife, or
the husband gone to work, the mother
a room away, child at her breast, swaddled
in the after-warmth of their night's accumulated
heat. Trust then, sure as the flare
of the wooden match.

In the open malevolence of this young
millennium, we are like lilies struck by snow:
asking why democracy works so well when
nothing's going wrong.
Why some lethal agreeableness chloroforms
the general will to dissent.

So much of reasoning
subtracts us from ourselves: *so far*
it is not us, nor anyone we know
whose liberty is traded out
for the general safety—illusionary oasis, *safety.*

My young fire-starter father
has done his work. The street he leaves
uncoils white plumes scribbling
the damp air, signs of life rising
from the chimneys of the wood-framed houses,
as if each had a comic-book voice for a comic-book
time in which war was going to succeed,
after which an eagle would sift down
into the hemlock, the men would come home
under confetti, and women, laying aside

their welding tools, would again disguise themselves
with aprons. A time in which horrors might
be stopped by the quick fix of war.

My flesh-and-blood father
glances back at the peace of his neighborhood
to which he has added one small, necessary magic: fire.
The lights are going on. Households are stirring.
The sweet wood-smoke nostalgia of democracy
hangs over the town.

for Leslie Bond (1907–1982)

and rise with the bird—
an old Irish saying meant to keep
the riverbank of the day: David's lambs
are grazing the lush green
of Ballindoon, green fortified
with limestone. When the man
is late a week to carry them
to market, I decide to save one.
For eighty euro I buy her back
from the slaughterhouse. *She
is white with a black head,*
Josie writes, *and sixteen mothers
are looking after her.* While
my country makes war, one lamb
is saved in the West of Ireland,
a sign to what oppresses, but a sign
of what? That in helplessness before
atrocities any innocence is oasis?

I drink from you, my lamb,
although I have never seen you.
But hearing they held you back,
how account for the white funnel
of joy you make on a bank of green
for no one's sake? My dusk
lies down with you a continent,
an ocean away. You are my army
of one, though your brothers and sisters
are gone to table. So are we all
bought and sold in the coin of the realm.

Lie down, my lamb, with the piteous
cries of your mothers. You are saved,
as surely as the bird will rise.
Saved and with no use
except to run free on a hillside,
peaceful and far from the horrors
of war, where sacrifice is shamed
by terms other than its own
pure gift. Lamb, I wish it were
otherwise, and my wish
is your life.
I've done the next-to-nothing I could.
As surely as that, we rise
with the bird.

What the New Day Is For

The marvel of day after night, after
sleep-travel in one place, after stretching
the body out—its surrender.
The marvel that sleep is not
the quicksand it seems
to the child, that the raft of it
carries us into morning, and that
whatever made us weep yesterday
has been strangely visited without us
and, its terms, though unrelentingly
the same, lift our night-changed hearts.

The new day has been given
so whatever befell us yesterday
can be withstood, not as it was,
but as if we had perished
into it, and, despite horror or joy,
something miraculous could be
done with us that surpasses even hope,
which only wants ascension of the prospect
and not the helpless, dire turn—its
clang and echo.

As the carriage horse
waits for the child's hand on its nose
or flank, memory awaits the new day,
wants to be stroked—to marvel that
with no engine except blood and bone or
a wondrous toss of mane and forelock—
the fable of the freshly given day

can carry not only itself, but
all those other days
that caused a horse and open carriage
to stand for what we remember
of the past in our midst.

So the new day in our presence is given
to pass unforgetting hands
before twin tunnels of breath flowing
through the horse's nostrils, sweet and warm
from a great moving oven that insists
that the dough rise, that somehow the hungry
be fed, and that a lost child, when it is
found living, despite the cold
of the mountain, assuages
as a balm and an abiding
beyond even the new day.

Not because a child
is so wonderful—whining and helpless and
freighted with unanswerable mother-love, but
because for reasons we don't stop
to understand, we have more mercy
for the child than the world has.
And we know this. For such knowing
makes spirits of us, sends the new day,
before which we are again ourselves,
and more. Having flickered against dread
we rise afresh, recomposed
by the many-chambered parameters
of the night releasing us.

Snow falls onto the lashes
of the carriage horse. Slow dark orbs
in their frosted caves of sight
stare down the wounds
of mere bodies, coax us out
as apparitions: what the new day
is for.

for Jiri, Lenka, and Alice in Prague

iv

Listen: a thrush at evening serenading the rain.

variation on a line by Hakuin

And I don't know why we are together, dear ghosts,
or why we have to part. Only that it is precious
and that I love this run-down subject.

from "Dear Ghosts,"

HEART-MIRROR

A little spit on the heart-mirror—
like my father, the gambler,
spitting into his palms
then rubbing them together
before he lets go
the dice. I am rolling
through stars
just thinking about it.
And my heart, rubbed clean
with maniac luck,
gets what it wanted
for once: this child's moon
and three sentinel lovers.

ORANGE SUTRA

I wanted to take you in, peel and all,
with the mind's all-swallowing.
But the mind prefers unoranging
the orange until a segment unhinges
to shine upright
in the night sky, unaware
of the night or of its own shining.

So the mind makes a darker thing
of night's conception of itself.
To be *at crescent* admonishes lamentation
as a temporary setback. Mindful
of the round, of the moon's fullness—the night,
encroaching, also draws power
to increase or disappear
into us, entirely.

Gone full again, how orange are you, Orange,
now that a moon mistakes you
for its daughter? Just as I thought: you are
a wisecrack in the abundance of night's spiraling
obituary, willing to carry us
with you like poor relations until
we run out of pretexts and gambits.

If I choose to live in mind of you,
I can know you only by a sideways glimpse,
the blackboard-staccato of a thought's mad
all-over grammar, those woolly bees
of the heart that want to sting a moment to death

with memory—spelling the past *wuz,*
with its fur on, and letting it roll before us
like an orange, a portable altar
that prays all over itself
with itself.

You could say so, Orange.
You could kneel as you said so.
The way an orange is always kneeling
and upright at once.

You Are Like That,

a moon, and then the night sky
around the moon, a violet-blue
made whole by phases
as the moon tries to submerge itself and
fails. Why do you pretend to go,
then surge back a slice at a time, just when
I've given you up? Sometimes fog washes in
from the strait and you are entirely
gone. What is it like to be
so *gone*? Do you feel my moth-mind fumbling
you up there in the dark?
I'm like the schoolgirl at the back of the class
who can't help raising her hand toward the ceiling
even when she can't answer
the question, lifting herself
by desire alone.

Do you care about questions? Or are you
both sides of the moon-coin now, subduing
even chance? One night in a car I raced
beside you up the mountains,
just to rise with you for once, instead of
like now, drifting toward my own night,
wondering if I can stay missing long enough
to discover sleep's lost, alternate door, the one
round as a moon with no threshold—
a door so open it's hard to find, even
when you do. Did passing through

happen something like that,
just because a dying occurred? or was dying itself
greedily restorative on its far side? or
was it better than any detective story: a charmed opening,
casual as a teacher pointing
to the lucky one who gets to erase
the blackboard, except for a few yellow half-
words at the top, which can only partly
be reached and so are freed to
float there for days like the left-over ghost
of a conjugation: *He was. I am.*

Open, like half of any-
thing: the way a tree,
even in a treachery of moon-
light, never worries about having enough
birds. Or, in the fullness of day-
light, that unspecific opening
that lets us import-
antly half-see
when the question, as it reaches,
knows it isn't
tall enough.

APPARITION

He's a boy walking across a field
in Seminole, Oklahoma—my uncle
who eventually came West, causing
my father to follow, then my mother, so I
would be born in the West.
Five years before he enters that field,
a brother, Clinton-G., falls—
having been sent up a tree to shake apples
down. His leg is broken and,
although penicillin exists, none
is given: there is poverty. It is
a far country place.

Befalls. His death befalls the family:
Clinton-G. dead of a broken leg.
But there he is five years later—walking
toward my uncle on his two good legs
in the story my uncle tells, as if
telling were a freshening of belief
that for seventy years refuses
to leave him.

He has been sent to the spring
with a bucket for water.
They have been picking cotton
all day in other fields, my uncle
and his five remaining brothers—my father
among them. *Picking until our fingers
bled,* my father said.

My uncle knows his dead brother
far off by his walk. *He was as close as*
you are to me, my uncle says. *He*
stood at the spring while I filled
the bucket. It was heavy then, and he
reached over and set his hand to
the wire handle beside mine, and we
carried that bucket of spring water
to the first rise before he
was gone and the full weight
of the water came onto my arm
again, so I had to stop
and pour half of it out to make it
the rest of the way
to the house.

Each time he tells me
he looks full at me—tears welling
where sorrow makes a form for itself, then
falls away. "*I saw Clinton-G.*" *I told*
them back at the house. But I just as well
said I'd met a terrapin
in the roadway. No one put any store
by it. I saw him alive
as I was, or maybe I had crossed over
and was lucky to get
back. I was sent for water many times after
and never saw him. Only the once.
Like birth. Like death. The once.
And he came back to no one
but me.

My uncle tells me this over a span
of years and, each time, I listen
like an apple shaken from a tree
by a dead child. I roll silently with it
a short distance,
then stop. Roll, the branch
still trembling above the fallen boy,
the fallen apples.

Or am I water to this story: poured out
to make the bucket light enough
to carry? Why was it so against witnessing
to volunteer even once to my uncle: *I believe you?*
Or was accompaniment intrusion, except by
the held-back words.

Sometimes a silence chooses you
in order to reverberate across time
like the wordless skeleton an apparition uses
to stand upright before the living,
and, in the stalwart way bone is
to breath—meant to be left importantly
behind, like spring water poured out. Belief
soaking in.

for Uncle Red

UNSPOKEN

Put a tight seal
on the heart, that leaky bucket.

The heart saved against speaking.
The one that doesn't speak at all.
The one that stands next to
                                    speaking.
Just that?

        Only that.

THE ROOSTER CROWS

in Bucharest and I am a child again
in the Port of the Angels. Our rooster is crooning
to the town. Time is malleable
as its cry: *Light*
is here! or even, *Light is coming!* since
when I go to the window
it is still dark.

Bucharest: city where a rooster dares
crow before sunrise. In America
some sleep-maddened executive
would have your head, would take you
down from these cobbled rooftops
where the invisible eyebrow above
the Brincovean window is bird song,
and the autumn rope of grapevine scrawls
the remains of a summer garden: *Why*

is the eye of that attic stuffed with newspaper?
Why is the house still empty
where the two brothers committed suicide?
Why did the beautiful childhood friend
grow up to go mad, to roar
at the world like a lioness? How
can such sweet pastry be made
where an old woman entirely in black stands
like the Black Queen on a marble chessboard
outside the swanky western-style supermarket?
She is starving and waits to be

noticed, as if her silence did not
rake the heart.

Little rooster, I'm glad you steal
sleep, my too comfortable dream-watching—
Why should I be allowed rest
when the open eye is the deep-sea-diving
of the soul? Liliana takes the milk we have bought
for our tea and gives it to the queen
whose blessing *Bodaproste, bodaproste!*
is a garland laid back for us
on behalf of our dead loved ones.

Little rooster, I hear your message—
The sun has teeth today! My angels at home
say, *There's a bite in the air,* as if harm
were disembodied and everywhere. Your cry
is teeth to me when I think of the man
Liliana tried to shield me from
at the celebration of Bucharest's patron saint,
St. Dimitrie—the man, so outwardly disfigured,
his features stretched across his skull
like the bowstring of fate, letting life
and death co-exist unforgettably in the scald
of our instant eye to eye.

I know that other meeting too—the gentle
look of kindness from the young bearded priest—how
does he keep sweetness, receiving what is
hard-to-reconcile from a beneficent God?

I hand him our list for prayers—our dead
in one column, living
in another. A strange bouquet, these offerings
from two sides of two worlds. His eyes
are fur to the soul. Two poets then, arm in arm
walking five hours through the streets of Bucharest,
going into shops where we don't buy anything
but think what everything we don't spend
would mean to someone alone
and hungry, or cold and sick.

What is happening to me, rooster?
My childhood as the woodcutter's daughter is as close
as your voice-star, sending its magical
spiked-with-hope-and-terror javelin.

There, below my window: the man
who makes brooms strides
through the street with fans of straw
under his arm, domestic spears against
disorder, against the debris of life's comings
and goings. He's calling softly, soothing
the household furies, saying he's here,
his brooms are ready to meet the pressure
of a woman's wrists, like those
in the church where the parishioner
sweeps the fallen petals of flowers
carried for miles from the countryside
by pilgrims. *Poor you,* Liliana says
to the woman, whose broom makes us lift
our feet above her offering.

Not at all, she answers, not
missing a stroke. *I do it for the grace of God.*

And what is that chucking sound just beneath
the hammering? I know it too.
My child hand reaches into the nest, enclosing
the egg—its warmth
like no other in the world.

BLACK BEAUTY

Pain added to pain it would have been,
to bring forward too soon
the beautiful unripe "us together" scenes.
So memory learned something from the dawn
about getting night out of the way,
letting dark be dark,
like the white heart of the apple
before it is broken open
to the miniature damp cathedral of its
even darker seeds.

There we are again
on the side-throne of the King Cole Bar
eating goblets of raspberries in February
at the St. Regis Hotel. This was between
renovations, after the skating rink, before
Lespinasse, and yes, it's true—the demolition
of that very room. Like memory, or at least
its corridor—the mural of the King at court survives—
dim channel through which bowls of raspberries
were once conveyed.

Where were these berries picked? we ask, spooning
them into our far away, snow-driven
mouths. *Mexico, Chile.* And we know
some twelve-year-old, or younger, has gathered
them, forty pounds per hour, down the cool
morning vines, a carrier strapped
to the waist, hands reaching, palms up
to catch any falling ripeness—then,

each berry grasped lightly between thumb
and fingers, given a turn—no jerk
or pull—to loose it from the vine.

I rest my spoon, watch Ray savor
our favorite fruit out of season,
like this poem written sixteen years after his death—
his 66th birthday. His pleasure is a red mountain
he scoops the top out of, like a crownless
king. Pleasure that had to traverse
unseemly diminishments and near deaths
to find his lips and tongue and teeth
in New York City, some publisher
footing our bills, making it
the sweeter, berries so red they are nearly
black, like that variety we never
got to sample: *Black Beauty,* said to be
"excellent and ever bearing." Like you.

A long way from Clatskanie
to this posh place! Our raw beginnings:
from the logging camps of the Olympic Peninsula or
yours in Yakima, the only house on the block with
an outhouse. No car so you walked everywhere,
your father filing saws at Boise Cascade, you
working the green chain like my brothers
in our mill town across state.

No wonder you can taste every one
of the 75 to 85 *druplets* in one
raspberry crown. If I were to tell you

these berries had escaped *root weevil, two-spotted*
tortrix, cane maggot, spur blight, gray mold, and even
a wart-like growth: *crown gall*—from bacteria
entering the plant through a wound—you
would just take the next bite
and say, *I believe it.*

One of the great things about living
longer, you said once, was *getting to learn more*
of the story. The details left by the visitor
to your grave, how a man's ashes were
stolen in an urn, along with a white Cadillac
convertible. The powdery remains jostled along
in the back seat with joyriders. The car
then torched so the ashes had to pass again
through fire, and twice refined, washed downstream,
the car nosed by then into a river.
Or maybe we retell it
so the ashes are still riding around
in that stolen car, coaching life's desperados.
In any case, the top is down, under
a cargo of stars.

Now you're talking, Ray says—delight
and the story going on into
the imperishable *now* of the never-again
raspberries he is consigning to his
one-and-only body beside me in that expansive,
gone-forever King Cole Bar.

Who said: *Raspberries do not keep*
or travel well? I'll stake my lot
with those ancient seafaring Chinese
who believed trees shed blood, or that to eat
the fruit of the 10,000 foot high Cassia tree
would make them immortal.

for Ray

Dream Doughnuts

Mother, I'm so glad
> *to see you again!* for she had been dead some while.
Oh my son! she says, kissing him, *I'm also glad*
> *to see you!*
I have so much to tell you, he says.
> *Tell me, then.*
Not now, mother, he says. *We have so much time.*

Pierre retells his dream at the Parisian restaurant
where Sebastian, the jazz musician
says he's going to give up drink,
take better care of himself. It's time
he *found a nice girl and settled down, had some*
children. Two young mathematicians at the table discuss logic
which I'm always hijacking with metaphor
and image. I tell them how I read Ray's
book of poems cover to cover until he entered
my dream as through some side-door in the jazz club,
some loophole in time.

I'm so glad to see you again, I say.
He's carrying a bag of powdered doughnuts
and two paper cups of black coffee.
Was I gone too long? he asks, fresh from the bakery.
Too long is if you don't come back at all, I say.
Time is funny, he says, biting into the doughnut
so the hole breaks open to the entire air supply
of the planet. Powdered sugar clings to the corners
of his lips. *Ghost-lips* I call him, as he
tears off doughnut and feeds it to me like a small bird

who won't eat any other way. Time,
like the doughnut hole, has rejoined itself,
as when joining breaks us open to ourselves, corollary
to *again.*

I say to Ray:

> *Did you ever think*
> *it would be like this?*
> *Drink your coffee,* he says, *while it's hot.*

For a while we're all out there together, but soon
I know I'll have to go back to that alcove
in which we're always waiting to see
each other again, the one we call Life, so it has
a hole in the middle, a sign of arrival, given
so we don't need to miss ourselves or anyone else,
we're that sure the whole,
in some unaccountable lightning-flash-hyphenation,
goes on and on, as it takes
our very breath away.

Urgent Story

When the oracle said, *If you keep pigeons*
you will never lose home, I kept pigeons.
They flicked their red eyes over me,
a deft trampling
of that humanly proud distance
by which remaining aloof
is its own fullness. I administered
crumbs, broke sky with them like breaking

the lemon-light of the soul's amnesia
for what it wants but will neither take
nor truly let go. How it revived me,
to release them! And at that moment of flight
to disavow the imprint, to tear
their compasses out by the roots of
some green meadow they might fly over
on the way to an immaculate freedom, meadow

in which a woman has taken off
her blouse, then taken off the man's flannel shirt
so their sky-drenched arc
of one, then the other above
each other's eyelids is a branding of daylight,
the interior of its black ambush
in which two joys lame the earth a while
with heat and cloudwork under wing-beats.

Then she was quiet with him. And he
with her. The world hummed
with crickets, bees nudging the lupines.

It is like that when the earth counts
its riches—noisy with desire,
even when desire has strengthened our bodies
and moved us into the soak of harmony.

Her nipples in sunlight have crossed his palm
wind-sweet with savor, and the rest
is so knelt before
that when they stand upright
the flight-cloud of my tamed birds shapes an arm
too short for praise.

Oracle, my dovecot
is an over-and-over nearer to myself
when its black eyes are empty.
But by nightfall I am dark
before dark if one bird is missing.

Dove that I lost from not caring enough,
Dove left open by love in a meadow,
Dove commanding me not to know
where it sank into the almost-night—for you
I will learn to play the concertina,
to write poems full of hateful jasmine and
longing, to keep the dead alive, to sicken
at the least separation.
Dove, for whose sake
I will never reach home.

V

Could it be that they taught solely through their spiritual presence, rather than through words?

Jiang Yuanliang
(on having a hard time
finding works by Buddhist nuns
for an anthology of poetry
in the mid-nineteenth century.
From *Daughters of Emptiness,*
translated by Beata Grant)

MOON'S RAINBOW BODY

Forbidden to travel by night,
you nonetheless arrive
at dawn. In Josie's portrait
I attend your birth moment,
accomplished in a swirl
of greens against a night sky
of green. Where did he
get you, green moon, and
by what permission do you
make a birth out of
a seeming disintegration?

Like a thumb print
on glass, you hover
in daylight, marking the sky
with a scar of midnight.
Suddenly my body leaps
with you into the immensity,
so gone the word *gone*
can't find a mouth
to say it. Each moonlit

arrival is like a gong
without a temple
reverberating against
an unseen mountain.
The spider's mouth
unravels a silken bridge
across which the fly
belies it ever
flew.

Dear Ghosts,

my friend is back from Cairo.
He is tired in the eyes from all he has seen.
Tired too from drinking whiskey straight
in the little dusty cafes, keeping up with the company.
It is 1991, before the bad business
of Iraq, before my own time in Cairo.

We drink a little whiskey together,
joining one far midnight to another, because
my black-haired orphan is with us—she whose brown eyes
add a crackling to the night. Her glances,
black butterflies of the general soul, join me to one
who is missing, who sleeps like a hive of wild honey
with his sweetness intact, like a blue door
sure and firm in the swift corridors
of the night. He who tries to wrest shards of love
from the world in broad daylight, who loves
only a little at first, then madly.

Love, such a run-down subject, says the ancient poet
of Rio. My orphan smiles and clicks
her whiskey glass to mine.

In Cairo the camels throw the weight of their haunches
onto their knees and rise up. An old man passes through
the cafe swinging from a chain his brass cylinder
embossed with stars and half-moons.
The charred droplets of burnt musk rain over us,

seep through our sleeves onto our skin.
My friend is talking about his Italian motorcycle.

Love, such a run-down subject, especially,
forced as I am, to mix these living creatures
with ghosts, with the axe-edge beauty
of a woman's indifference and the sleeping lips
of that one who lies even more deeply asleep in me.

Suddenly the bar is noisy, the music
a raw throb at the base of the brain. We can't talk
about love or anything else in here. Time
to put our arms around each other's waists—my man,
my woman, my unapproachable dream.
Time to walk out into the pungent streets of Cairo
with kisses of good night on a street corner
where it is dark and cool enough
for weddings that happen all night long
to the frantic pulse of the *tabla*. Move back, the men
are dancing, the men are showing their sex
in their hips, their bellies and waists. Rose water
is splashing our brows on this street corner, unappointed
as we are, but bound inexactly by whiskey,
loud music, Italian motorcycles, by the unknown
parents of my orphan.

And in the wide silence of each step,
the implosive blue rose drops unknowingly
into my thigh to preserve love's ache, love's

incandescent whisper under the black smell of mountains.
And I don't know why
we are together, dear ghosts, or why
we have to part. Only that it is precious
and that I love
this run-down subject.

EMANATION OF THE RED CHILD

Child that never existed
because to exist
is to need the world
as a place merely to enter
as a leaving. Child
the horse's legs stepped through
crossing the river; how you kept
the red of you in the river-flow
so as always to be seen, the not-sure
of you gathering, undulating
edgeless and the rider
swinging down from the stirrup
to stand waist high in you
as you dissipated and reformed
like a fish flexing its
river-muscle. Child pulling light
into a tattered guess-work shawl
under trees. Spirit-shout
whose echo refuses its assignment
of incremental leave-taking and so
gains stature, agreeing to stay
fringed with loss just glancing
off promise. We enter the inexplicable
where the child's delight exceeds
what can be seen by anyone looking on.

So the red child exceeds our thought
of it, envelopes eagerly the shimmering
notion of the horse's nostrils sifting its
water-garden of breath-lilies where

no birth can empty it and no death
ever drink its fill. Red child
finding a way to be and not be
like a riderless horse
letting the river fall from its flanks
as it gains the bank
and its horse-mind catches the glint
of light in water where a stirrup,
the steely brand of it marks
the red-child-moment
and is empty, so empty
we keep on seeing
what can't be
seen.

for Tiernan

CAIRO MOON

Climbing down into, or stories up
inside the pyramids. Plush violet-chill.
Tombs emptied of treasure, of mummified
monkeys and the sleek cats of pharaohs. My driver
Ali—once bodyguard to Anwar Sadat—grips
my hands to protect, his silence more daring
for companioning an uncloaked woman.
Never look only straight ahead—what he learned
avoiding the assassin, his head gliding turret-like
in a slow arc, left to right, then back.

So far from earth we are—our scant scraps
of language implode the signals: life into
death, into the quick gaze he gives me
as in some ancient calm, sending permission
to be happy in this moon-shorn impossibility,
this tall cave of never.

In the cafe only men that afternoon,
their *sheesh* pipes gurgling, the caftaned owner
doing sums in the corner. We drink thick sweet
coffee from small hot glasses.
Something of the tomb's intimacy still clings, binds
my arms to my sides, lashes me to the prow
of myself, self that sails away
as someone eternally awake
on an unreachable horizon. I am like that
and like that, and we say
next to nothing. Then, *Pasha, that's what
I'll call you,* he says,
in the pearl of the moment.

During the day, white brain-boiling heat.
Hooded women so beautiful the slit
of their eyes makes a beacon when they turn
their solid light-house forms into
the dusty street.

Ali takes me to meet his recently widowed mother.
Softly near me, his second wife, draped
in golden silk. Their two children—kisses,
firm petals against my face, my lips,
and his son's brown eyes dancing.
I drink Pepsi from a tray, sit alone
with the widow who lets me
try her ring with its black triangular stone.
Is it her husband's gift?
We are in the lost language
of show-but-can't-tell. Showing
as offering. Her sad slow eyes.
Her brave empty finger—my own
unsettled hand where, for a moment,
the black stone of our dead reigns.

In the street Ali's son does circles on his bike,
going to get bread, but waving, waving
as I climb into the jeep,
as if I were sailing distantly away,
even as I gaze back, raise my hand,
wave this ongoing good-bye.

I can spot Ali in the night by the swing
of his shoulders. What torch, what
tower am I then? Walking bareheaded
into the violet dazzle of a night so deep
the moon holds me, for a moment, above myself—until
my heart is not my heart, but something inward
and golden with an unknown strength.

I am rearranged from the cells out, having passed
so near the tracings, the musk of workers' hands
on chiseled granite inside the pyramids. Did they
enter my body in that space designed to preserve flesh
into some eternal use?
There is a moon over us
that could swallow the planet. And I hate my dead heart,
banished by a city so more-than-alive, so shining and eager
to bear the pilfering come-and-go
of robbers.

Sleep on, Pharaohs,
on whatever shelf you rest in the great museum
of golden needles and miniature
water jars. Pasha is set on earth again, for a while,
and walks, as in life given back to life,
under the relentless blue sky of one moment in Egypt,
the yellow dust of the pyramids sifting
into her sandals, an alchemy, silken and bare enough
for the journey.

Tomorrow is supposed to be the anniversary of my death,
Tomorrow I am supposed to have been alive—
once upon a time.

Shiraishi Kazuko
("The Anniversary of Smansa's
Death," translated by Kenneth
Rexroth and Ikuko Atsumi)

Across the Border

Into early morning we circle
the problem of his mother's dementia,
her cries of *help me! help me!*
ricocheting against the stars
even from the balcony of this posh hotel
across the Canadian border
where he and his family are like refugees
of some secret war-torn country
within the country. I sit with him
the way a mountain sits with another
mountain, comparing weather,
the slippage of glaciers, the racket of
helicopters searching for lost
climbers, anything that spoils our
violet reveries with the night.

His hope-coffers are empty.
She doesn't know who he or anyone else
is. She thrashes wall to wall like
a trapped bird. No one wants to help
him take care of her—the waiting lists
at the facilities up to a year.
I need something, she tells him, *but
I can't tell you what it is.*

She hasn't slept for days.
The medicine that opens the sleep door
doesn't work on her. The anti-psychotics
don't tamp down the fear anymore.
She's like watching a lightning storm

over a lake, doubled and single-minded
at once. No comforting arms
for her. She won't be placated. She's
a force now, like wind or rip tide
uttering unanswerable edicts as it
dashes things to pieces. He dashes
each suggestion I make. Too late
for that. Or that.

Now we know why the old women
are lighting candles in the dark alcove
of the church, kindling a wavering city
of light, white candle burning next to white
candle. Maybe that's the trace hope leaves
when it's emptied out by crude events—reduced
to a sign, a silent cry made of light.

for Greg

She Wipes Out Time

like shaking horseflies from her white mane.
She would like to mail a postcard to
the place she was born. Not just to anyone,
but to the postmaster. *When I stopped to*
see him he'd gone out into his fields.
He had forty acres, she says. *I didn't*
go looking for him. I gaze across America, across
death to the postmaster, walking
his Missouri fields—wide sweep of farmland,
walnut groves, rivers and once-inhabited Indian caves
gouged into hillsides I explored
as a child by horseback.

A thousand acres, my mother says, restoring
them to herself and bequeathing them
to her children. *Your grandfather has a thousand acres.*
That sentence still a kingdom. The land gone,
but the words of it sustaining,
as if those acres—the vibratory memory
of them—were somehow currency to feeling able
for an expanse of loss. But who needs
a thousand acres? Better to have the thought
without the bother, to walk the mind under walnut trees
on the slope behind a barn long since
fallen away—as the mind falls away—the roots
exposed so the dry tendrils of small bushes
that cling bird-footed to air
remind us that air itself is a soil
apparitional to desire.

I too want to go back. Do go,
through the long stride of her wish
to make this sign of remembrance: a postcard
to the postmaster. In my mother's memory
of home, on which I lean, the postmaster still walks
his forty acres, though I know he is
long dead. Is it cruel to tell her
and obliterate that switchback
her yearning makes to resurrect him—who now
represents a place she can't quite reach
in her mind, except through the hyphenated corridor
of his perpetual looming up
as one broken promise?
I said I'd stop and see him . . . calm disappointment
in her voice. Any god would let this postmaster
have his saunter in the mind-works of another. I say
nothing, let him live, beckoning to us both
across time, death and any upstart moment
that chooses her.

I am attracted to this new fold in time
by which a postmaster escapes death through having
gone for a walk. But I want her with me.
"Mother," I ask, "when did you last see him?"
Her voice has the lilt of truth. Memory's strange accordion
crumples expertly under the tail of the monkey:
Oh, a couple years ago.
"Mother, it's twenty years since you were back."
Then, making her arrow sing: *How time flies!*

By custodial violence I yank her to my template,
offer the card she wanted to send.
She forgets what it was for, uses it all day
as a page marker in her handbook
on African violets. Later she
reads deliciously aloud: *Water them*
from the top and you'll rot the crown. Always
let them take what they need
from the bottom.

Language itself has flown
defensively from the page into her
mouth with the audacity of particulate, unquenchable
matter that is, at any moment, fully able
to restore girlish laughter
to the high veranda, the postmaster's hand
closing vast distances
to my father's courtship letters,
ten years handing them over to her—letters
from her lover, far away in the desperate burrowings
of the coal mines. And now depths darker.
Twenty years toiling under us in the black ore of absence,
as the violets drink on their sills
from little bowls of the mind.

for Georgia Marie Morris Bond

The Violence of Unseen Forms

". . . oh how I long just once to feel
the hand within me that throws larks so high into the sky"
letter from Rilke

Can one soul consume
another? Or does asking violate
the notion: soul inviolable?
To ask is to wonder anew at the violence
of unseen forms.

Was it will over will?
Or did superior need bend us, one to
another? Does one who serves
hold the upper hand, having failed purposefully,
in the small ways, to mark and seal
parameters?

Is there loss?
Or does the soul-inside-the-soul
resort to bird song, to the shadow-languages
of touch and glance at its central core,
preferring undertow as it
more graciously attends
the world's day by day.

When one soul takes on the heft
of a faltering soul
is it transaction, translation, atonement
or all three—for which the deeds themselves
are gratefully forfeit
to the renewed essence of both?

All I know is, when her soul
seemed to fail her, I had no choice.
In the lifting up I became another
venturing, could shake far cries in realms
unguessed. Nor could I return
without the shade of her
who carried me into her need, beyond
mere mercies.

Only then did the deeper hand in me
learn to throw larks
for sheer pleasure: to feel them climb sky
to heights never touched otherwise,
and for no reason. Just, inexplicably, we could.
And with that release
the violence, against all prediction,
ended.

BEHAVE

Central word of my childhood.
A father's plea that could turn
command, then verge on threat: *behave,*
I want you to behave now.
Word, tender enough
over years to slice distance
into the two halves of any question—
his authority gauged in
backward glances or met
like a freight train loading up
its reasons. *If you don't behave . . .* he'd say,
desperation mounting against the din
of household to let him, after the day's labor,
find some riverbank-moment where stillness
could come, could eddy, then release
him into his *far away*—that place
we could sense him wanting
to get back to, like a drowning man
whose life seems the far shore
when it is a breath at the lip
of a watery precipice under him.

Roethke, other long-gone father,
paraphrasing Marianne Moore to tell us:
once we feel deeply we begin to behave.
The notion of right action proceeding
naturally out of right feeling—
poetry the witching stick, not only
to what was felt, but how *the ability to feel a thing*
is already something done to the good.

I stand at last near his grave in Saginaw
with Kunitz in mind, give over
conjoined years of learning to behave as empathy,
turncoat of prejudice and dismissal. Empathy—art's
sloe-eyed handmaiden: wearing in the marrow
the strictness, the necessary solitude, the passion
of that mandate. Still, beside the instructing presence
of the dead—I do, in my own way, behave.
Roethke's great love of poetry
claims me afresh. With only my life
I've told him, that for the spiritual child
there *are rights in the matter,*
that the heart of those first ungainly poems
he more than read still practices
the ongoing restoration
a life in poetry can be.

To good purpose the remaking
of language gradually teaches, enfolds
and leads to tenderness—despite
the steely hammer blows that fall as if
the life too were steel,
when it is only that child in a doorway, that father
at the table, head in his hands,
and the word *behave* finding me so audibly
I bend to the grave, grateful to take,
with each poem, a breath
from its carnation before giving it
to stone.

for Stanley Kunitz, Theodore Roethke, Leslie Bond

OIL SPOT

A blue-black planet, it falls from
the chainsaw into rainwater
puddled where the earthquake
left its shoulders in the driveway,
the depression in gravel
reminding us we walk on waves.

The droplet flings itself down, radiates
like a jellyfish unfurling its
mantle—filtrating, rippling.
At its core, a violet eye,
magenta-lashed, its milky skirting
buoyant.

Josie goes into the house
for the camera to take its portrait.
The door to beauty always
stands open. Days later he stares
at the photograph until it enters
him fully, just a spot of oil,
transforming his hand
with its paint brush
into an instrument of rainbow
approximations that begin to pale
the original.

Like a satellite moon
the eyelet center deeply shines.
Planet-Josie revolves over
it, the light of his face

also entering as he works.
Beauty passes through us
blackly shuddering, stabilizes
its revolution and, against
all expectation, begins to rise from
the undulating shape
on his page.

A heart like that
at eighty

for Josie Gray, b. March 23, 1925

CULTIVATION

She said she had made the garden
for the garden. Not her own pleasure.
Flowers. The wildest I ever saw.

In Lilac-Light

That's what poems are for,
unlivable love.

notebook entry

She is so eager for any emerging
sign of spring, she cuts the stems in bud,
tight seeds before scent that will push open
four-pronged lavender fists,
what she makes visible of her deep will
to live. She places them like the bowed heads
of sea horses in the glass pitcher *to drink*
while we talk.

The mystery novel someone loaned
lies unread on the table. And why not?
She lives the more-than-mystery
of last days. Time-gone, like giddy
mountain air, has expanded her gaze—its
great stillness, its focus
without center.

Scent of lilacs to come.
Scent of lemon and coriander
from the meal I've carried to her
in the cast-iron skillet. She lights
the swirled golden candlestick
given by an enemy, yet saved
for a special occasion. All are
special now. Its flame leaps to air.
In lilac-light even enemies
grow benign.

Hooves strike long sparks
on the cobblestones of memory.
She talks about Margie, the little gray mare
she rode to school through snow seventy
and more years ago. "Give me a horse today,
I could ride it!" she says.

How air-blue we are with dusk
coming on, the Celtic whisper—*duskus*
Josie names it, so we embody the *us* of dusk,
plea and surrender, to which we are
a violet inner chamber.

My mother steps through a doorway
in Leadmine, Missouri—lilacs
in her hands, where my young father,
celebrating his birthday, sees a woman
whose waist-length hair sweeps the room
so he must ask, as in a fable,
Who is that black-haired woman?
He does not look away from where she
stands and stands the rest of his lifetime,
holding to the singe of their locked embrace,
its blackened rim of purpose, of room-dulled passion
whose release I am.

Dusk, papery husk of night
before night, let me have one wish
on the brink of a speaking silence: not
to betray their story which, like the scent
of lilacs, comes from outside itself, the lie and lack
so unerringly mixed, daughter and mother are
one breath, descending into this gradual
over-sweet eviction.

Consider the Resurrection or the night when Jesus walked on water. On neither occasion did he appear before his disciples in a "ghostly" spiritual body; it is reported that he was present with them in the flesh.

John Hutchison
("Walking on Water" in *Clouds,*
a publication associated with the
paintings of Patrick Hall shown
in 2002 at Butler Gallery, The
Castle, Kilkenny, Ireland)

WATER WALKING

Jesus is walking
on the water.
He is not ghostly.
He is not gauzy
with spirit. Otherwise
the fleshly water could not
perform the miracle of bearing up
the equally fleshly man.

A jet passes over
the secluded valley cottage.
Josie looks up and says it's
hard to believe three hundred people
are sitting up there
in the air.

Jesus walks and walks.
His real feet are bare
as the water is bare.
When he reaches the boat and
climbs in, Thomas will dry his feet
with a cloth. The cloth will be
hung up to dry in the corporeal wind.

The challenge is not about
Thomas's doubts or the transcendence
of the spirit, but about the earthly
body, the perishable notion of it
as it exactly sustains each earthly action: to walk

on water as water, demonstrating
that we hardly know under what terms
we perform our sitting in air, our miraculous,
perilous stepping out in the flesh
over the everyday void.

I Asked That a Prayer

be offered at his grave,
though we were awkward about it,
exposed to do so, there on the cliffside
above the strait. I remembered how once
Ray asked friends to offer thanks at a meal
because he knew they did it
when he wasn't there.

I already had my eyes closed,
because that's how I learned to pray
as a child. This made a voice
of the prayer and of the world.
The voice said: *the prayer will be a moment*
of silence in which we each
offer up a prayer.

Silence then.
And, while we were in the middle of it, wind
rushed like a hand over the chimes
above the stone.
I thought: *he's here!*
and so did everyone else.
We even spoke about it
afterwards. Let ourselves know.
That's how he came to be
with us, through a moment
as its own speaking.

I heard all of him
in that broken-open

eternity—bright metal
fumbling sea air.
Then the wild precipice of peace
in which earth itself
falls away.
The silence
after the silence.

SURGEON

He's sketching the shape
of the incision across my left
breast. *What about my heart?*
I can't help asking.
*Oh, don't worry. We'll leave
that.* He smiles.
A *bat wing* he calls the design
he'll use to lift the breast from
the chest wall. *Thanks, doc,
for giving me half my boyhood
back,* I tell him from the gurney,
thinking to relieve his scalpel
of hesitation. Then I'm under.

Afterwards, high on pain meds,
I talk on the phone
to loved ones in an exuberant
soaring and don't recall a thing.
Strange to put my hand
there days later and find only
the pouting lip.

Suzie tending the wound
after my night's respite
in hospital. She's left her easel
to minister. Alfredo up and
down from the basement where
he's been painting dream-jungles,

checking on me, asking sweetly
in his own healing mantra:
Tessita-how-you <u>do</u>-ing?

My third operation in a year and
Suzie's confident now, knows
how to manage this. Like a bewildered
child, I surrender to comfort
when she tucks me in at night.
Don't talk to me of heaven.

for Susan Lytle and Alfredo Arreguín

THE RED DEVIL

the nurses on the cancer ward call it
because, like acid, if it spills
from the needle onto skin, the patient
has to have a skin graft. Red devil
for how it singes the inside of
the veins, causes the hair to fall
out and the nails of the hands and feet
to lift from their beds, to shrivel
or bunch like defective armor.

Now the test reveals the heart
pumps 13% less efficiently.
Never mind. Your heart
was a superheart anyway.
Now it's normal. Join
the club. Get tired. Learn to nap.
Watch the joggers loping uphill
as if under water, as if
they had something to teach you
about the past, how sweet
and useless it was, taking the stairs
two at a time. They still
call you *hummingbird.*
Sooner or later you'll be flying
on your back to prove
you've got at least
one trick left.

SKY HOUSE

In all the sunny climes
the houses like to be dark
because shadow gives refuge.
My house is made of light
I loved too much
to tear from the whole. I rise
into the day like a fish, mottled briefly
in the shallows by something over-
hanging, then dart silver
into silver, past the quick
of the moment into
all time, moving as one fish
with the spine of another
in its forever-opened
mouth. I don't worry where
it's taking me
or seek shelter, or any of the other
holding-patterns
of the soul—I'm that light-
possessed, in-
side the *in.*

BUDDHA ALCOVE

Friends are leaving after tea.
The water-welcome, splashed
from the bucket before they came,
has dried from the stones.
One more thing! One more, I say.
Follow me! It's Yosha, their child,
who understands, and whose presence
lends invitation. I lead them through
the hint at an opening in bamboo
to a fir and hemlock cave.

A hush falls.
We're in sacred space
with one *sitting stone* and two
watching stones. The mottled light
of the *money tree* thatches the air
over us. Bird song is clarified, more
otherworldly but also *this* world
and none other. The voices
of neighborhood children ripple
like a river through us.

All those times I quietly sat here
to bring the world into its
full shelter, its immense
stillness at center.
How did you make this place? they ask,
uneasy with the inner surround of it.
They attribute too much to me. Yosha
folds himself comfortably

onto the ground. He is the child-bridge
by which illumined mind
can enter.

I stumbled onto it, laying down mulch.
It was here a long time before I found it.

They're headed back to the world
after a Canadian holiday,
and the alcove makes them sweetly
nostalgic. It changes our speech, causes us
to whisper like children hiding
in the broom closet from parents.
I tell them how I slept here one night,
despite cougar warnings. Despite the snap
of fall in the air. The voices of owl
and coyote came on duty. Fragrance
of fir tree mixed with hemlock
in the dark—took some getting used to,
as if I'd shared my bed
with a rustling white presence,
so tenderly over me I was
twice awake. Quail nesting
farther up in the branches
rustled, chucked domestically
as they settled, and the tree
went back to being a tree.

All night I slept on the plush of leaves
fallen year upon year. The moon
found its way into my thicket

and woke me. That's when
I noticed the lights of my house
left on, and had the notion of possible alarm,
should the interval of absence
go on longer.

I was only a cosmos away.
I let the lights burn and the worrying-one
range her rooms like a bereft mother.
In the morning I heard geese flying south
from Canada. It takes so long
to figure out how to live.
I didn't worry for them. Just marveled
at the impetus of their journey
passing over, lifting me into
the incalculable day.

My guests heard me out,
but clearly this night apart
made them lonely, as if
someone else, another
they could not know
had returned.

for Yosha

BULL'S-EYE

Driving to the ferry,
that reverie releasing
the unsaid, I tell my friend
it's okay. I'll be okay.
When the doctor
said *There's no cure*
an arrow flew out of
the cosmos—*thung!*
Heart's center. Belonging
to everything. That
quick.

for Valerie

REMAINS

The relatives, giddy with abandon,
tell how they mixed ashes,
a father's with a mother's, saved
for that occasion, then
sifted them from their hands into
the Strait of Juan de Fuca.

I hear it often now, the old ways
of my farming ancestors, the body
going into the earth whole,
put aside for ash
into wind.

Don't worry,
I console my own. *I'll find a way*
to scatter you
even under the earth.
The planet is teeming with
neighborly help.

With Setouchi-san in Kyoto

We are like two sisters separated at birth.
We giggle with delight in each other's presence.
After a while we turn to talk
of love so perfected when the husband dies
it isolates. But I've gone on nonetheless
to love again. Setouchi-san
explains the plight of widows
in Japan whose families bury them
alive, for they cannot begin anew.

The tape recorder is on. Our words
are like distant rain. *One cannot mourn*
forever, even when one mourns
forever. The heart finds a chink
in the dark. I give her my late love
as example, as permission.
If one widow brightens,
a cosmos ignites.

Setouchi-san's belief in love
is my passport. We lock
little fingers, sealing a promise
that next time she'll come to me.
We know the odds
are against it. But even vows
that can't be enacted are important.
Her fervent wish spires

the moment. After long illness, easy
to think we may never see
each other again.
But fervency says otherwise,
says: *this side, or that.*

for Setouchi-san, for Hiromi

WALKING MEDITATION WITH
THICH NHAT HANH

Fifty of us follow him loosely
up the mountain at Deer Park Monastery.
We are in the slow motion of a dream
lifting off the dreamer's brow. Steps
into steps and the body rising out
of them like smoke from a fire
with many legs. Gradually the flames
die down and the earth is finally under us.
Inside the mountain a centipede crawls
into no-up, no-down.

Our meditations
waver and recover us, waver
and reel us in to our bodies
like fish willing at last to take on the joy
of being fish, in or out of the water.
When we gather at last at the summit
and sit with him
we know we have moved the mountain
to its top as much as it carried us
deeply into each step.

Going down is the same.
We breathe and step. Breathe,
and step. A many-appendaged being
in and out of this world. No use

telling you about peace attained.
Get out your feet.
Your breath. Enter
the mountain.

for Holly

Sixteenth Anniversary

You died early and in summer.

Today, observing the anniversary
alone in a cabin at La Push,
I wandered down to the gray-shingled
schoolhouse at the edge of the sea.
A Quileute carver came out of a low shed.
He held classes in there, he said. Six
students at a time. He taught me
how to say "*I'm going home*"
in Quileute by holding my tongue in
one side of my cheek,
letting the sounds slur past it, air
from the far cheek
a kind of bellows.

I felt an entirely other
spirit enter my body. It
made a shiver rise up in me
and I said so. The carver
nodded and smiled. He
said he taught carving
while speaking Quileute.
I imagined that affected
the outcome, for the syllables
compelled a breath in me
I'd never experienced before.

He showed me a rattle
in the shape of a killer whale
he'd been carving. The tail
had split off, but he said he
could glue it back. He let me
shake it while he sang
a rowing song they used
when whaling. My whole arm
disappeared into the song;
the small stones inside
the whale kept pelting
the universe, the sound
raying out into the past
and the future at once,
never leaving the moment.

He told me his Quileute name,
which he said didn't mean
anything except those syllables.
Just a name. But I knew he
preferred it to any other. "I'm going
home," I said, the best I could
in his language, when
it was time to walk on
down the beach. Fog
was rolling in so the rocks
offshore began to look
conspiratorial. He offered
his hand to shake. Our
agreement, what was it?
Wordless. Like what

the fog says when it
swallows up an ocean.
He swallowed me up
and I swallowed him up.
And we felt good about it.

You died early and in summer.

Before heading to the cemetery
I made them leave the lid up
while I ran out to the garden
and picked one more bouquet
of sweet peas to fan onto your
chest, remembering how you
beamed when I placed them
on your writing desk in
the mornings. You'd draw
the scent in deeply,
then I'd kiss you on the brow,
go out, and quietly close
the door.

We survive on ritual, on
sweet peas in August, letting
the scent carry us, so at last the door
swings open and we're both
on the same side of it
for a while.

If you were here we'd
sit outside, accompanying

the roar of waves
as they mingle with the low notes
of the buoy bell's plaintive warning,
like some child blowing
against the cold edge of a metal pipe.
I'd tell you how the Quileute
were transformed from wolves
into people, though I'm unsure
if they liked the change. I'm
not the same myself, since
their language came into me.
I see things differently.
With a wolf gazing out.
I can't help my changes any more
than you could yours. Our life apart
has outstripped the mute kaleidoscope
of the hydrangea and its seven changes.
I'm looking for
the moon now. We'll have
something new
to say to each other.

Aug. 2, 2004
for Raymond Carver
and for Chris Morgenroth, Quileute Nation

COMEBACK

My father loved first light.
He would sit alone
at the yellow formica table
in the kitchen with his coffee cup
and sip and look out
over the strait. Now,
in what could be
the end of my life, or worse,
the life of someone I love, I too
am addicted to slow sweet beginnings.
First bird call. Wings
in silhouette. How the steeples
of the evergreens make a selvage
for the gaunt emerging sky.

My three loves are far away
in other countries,
and one is even under
this dew-bright ground
where the little herds
of jittery quail peck
and scurry for their lives.

My father picks up his
cup. Light is sifting in
like a gloam of certainty
over the water. He knows
something there in the half light
he can't know any other way.

And now I know it with him: so much
is joining us in the dawn
that no one can ever be parted.
It steals over us because we left
the warm beds of our dreams
to sit beside what rises.
I think he wants to stay there
forever, my captain, gazing but not
expecting, while the world
begins, and, in a stark silent calling,
won't tell anyone what it's for.

DEATH'S INK

like petroleum or toothpaste, comes
in viscous suspensions, watery seepage,
or the fatefully indelible.
A serious, too serious poet tried to fill the pen
as often as possible from its rollicking vein.
For like a heft of sea in calm, we bless
ourselves in knowing what's under us,
that it is deep and cold and uncontrollable.

A young poet, far from death, I wanted
to scrawl green ink over all that happened,
as if to inoculate a future I could not see.
When friends died, I ran to memory
like a second mother, shoring up
with a blurry nib a glimpse, some jaunty
cock of hat or squint into light on water.

What my father said one day
when we were driving: *I've broken every bone
in my body.* I wrote that down on the back
of a water bill. Also the story my friend Keiko
told of orphaned Japanese babies
handed over to the Chinese to save, wrapped
in moss-blue silk or wearing some handmade
garment, no other sign of where they'd come from.

Fifty years they clung to the shreds of their
swaddling clothes like identity cards,
still searching for their parents.
This too, saved with death's ink, because death

is the haven of hapless searchings—lost babes,
lost fathers and mothers, the washed-out ink
of their names that leaves them invisibly written
into time, as it runs out, and the valiance
of the search is all that's left, or the pen
scratching the tree inside the paper
to emboss moonlight on forest ferns
or on the snowy vault
of Mt. Olympus—the eyelet step

of a deer. Ink that is a laceration
in the dream of morning, our waking
to sunlight glinting offshore of the mind.
Ink I follow like a trail of bird song,
stepping over dead soldiers, over
entire kingdoms, over stars
dead or waiting to be quenched.
For only with death's eggshell nimbus
around each word could I break through
life's greedy confinement and discover
the impudent clot each period insinuates,
a rest stop for death, holding back syntax

until meaning catches up.
Until the babes cross the border of
held-back-time and a swatch of cloth
brightens memory's jaguar eye. Nothing
matches the undiscovered embrace
of those who remain unrecognized.
Death's ink loves them more. And my father's
broken bones are mended underground

because I recall his handsome swagger, his skill
at cards, his fearless venturing to top a tree
eighty feet from earth. I loan to life
this blooded ink that agrees to pass out of time
without loss or memory, having given over in tatters
the spirit I ransacked like a despot.
So the period falls with a clang.
And all goes on—

Tess Gallagher is the author of seven previous volumes of poetry, including *Moon Crossing Bridge* and *Amplitude: New and Selected Poems*. She is also the author of *Soul Barnacles: Ten More Years with Ray, A Concert of Tenses: Essays on Poetry,* and two collections of short fiction, *At the Owl Woman Saloon* and *The Lover of Horses and Other Stories*. She lives and writes in Port Angeles, Washington.

The text of *Dear Ghosts,* has been set in ITC New Baskerville, a typeface designed by Matthew Carter and John Quaranda in 1978, and inspired by the work of John Baskerville (1706–1775), an accomplished writing master and printer from Birmingham, England.

Book design by Wendy Holdman. Composition by Prism Publishing Center. Manufactured by Maple Vail Book Manufacturing on acid-free paper.

√